My Dinosaurs

by Anne Giulieri
photography by Ned Meldrum

Here are my dinosaurs.

This dinosaur is big.

This dinosaur is little.

My big dinosaur

is looking at the water.

My big dinosaur goes in the water.

7

My little dinosaur
is looking at the water.

My little dinosaur
goes in the water, too!

My little dinosaur
is on the rocks.

Can you see it?

My big dinosaur
is in the leaves.

Can you see it?

My little dinosaur
is in the grass.

Can you see it?

You can play, too!